Be Free

Writing Prompts for the Mind, Body, and Soul

———————

Yvelette Stines

Author: Yvelette Stines
Editor: Bettina Ortez
Designer: Ashlee Chesny

Dedication

This book is dedicated to the people who are working hard to make their dreams come true. Keep the faith.

Gratitude

With humility I thank God, my family, friends, supporters,
community, and ancestors.

*Yves Stines, Bettye Stines, Bettina Ortez, Joshua Ortez, Kinyel
Friday, Niki Johnson, Julie D. Andrews, Dr. Linda Selim, Dr.
LeConte Dill, Dr. Elaine Carey, Gwen Jimmere, Elizabeth
Whittaker-Walker, Charlena Ponders, Francina James, Rebecca
Rudnicki, Louise Spector and Ashlee Chesny.*

Introduction

Writing is a spiritual practice that can help you create a beautiful relationship with yourself. Many people want to write, but they are not sure how to begin. Writing prompts are a wonderful way to start and/or continue a writing practice and write with ease.

This book is a series of prompts that focuses on the mind, body, and soul. With each prompt, blank pages, lined pages, numbered lines, and boxes. Please use the space you feel most connected to. With the extra space, you can always come back to the prompts and see the shifts and growth with your writing practice.

Enjoy the book and your writing journey.

Peace and blessings,

Yvelette Stines

Mind

WRITING PROMPTS FOR THE MIND

What makes you feel alive?

What makes you feel alive?

1.

2.

3.

4.

5.

What makes you feel alive?

What makes you feel alive?

What steps do I need to take for my peace of mind?

What steps do I need to take for my peace of mind?

1.

2.

3.

4.

5.

What steps do I need to take for my peace of mind?

What steps do I need to take for my peace of mind?

What happened when you decided to get out of
your own way?

What happened when you decided to get out of your own way?

1.

2.

3.

4.

5.

What happened when you decided to get out of your own way?

What happened when you decided to get out of your own way?

What is a past narrative that no longer serves me?

What is a past narrative that no longer serves me?

1.

2.

3.

4.

5.

What is a past narrative that no longer serves me?

What is a past narrative that no longer serves me?

What do I need to release in my life in order to move forward?

What do I need to release in my life in order to move forward?

1.

2.

3.

4.

5.

What do I need to release in my life in order to

move forward?

What do I need to release in my life in order to
move forward?

What emotion is stopping me from getting started on my dreams?

What emotion is stopping me from getting started on my dreams?

1.

2.

3.

4.

5.

What emotion is stopping me from getting started on my dreams?

What emotion is stopping me from getting started on my dreams?

What brings me joy?

What brings me joy?

1.

2.

3.

4.

5.

What brings me joy?

What brings me joy?

What is stopping me from making the decision that will bring me happiness?

What is stopping me from making the decision that will bring me happiness?

1.

2.

3.

4.

5.

What is stopping me from making the decision that will bring me happiness?

What is stopping me from making the decision that
will bring me happiness?

What are three to five ways that I can improve the

conversations that I have with myself?

What are three to five ways that I can improve the
conversations that I have with myself?

1.

2.

3.

4.

5.

What are three to five ways that I can improve the

conversations that I have with myself?

What are three to five ways that I can improve the conversations that I have with myself?

What are some self-sabotaging habits that I need to

release?

What are some self-sabotaging habits that I need to release?

1.

2.

3.

4.

5.

What are some self-sabotaging habits that I need to release?

What are some self-sabotaging habits that I need to

release?

What will make you fearless?

What will make you fearless?

1.

2.

3.

4.

5.

What will make you fearless?

What will make you fearless?

What do you fear most about your future?

What do you fear most about your future?

1.

2.

3.

4.

5.

What do you fear most about your future?

What do you fear most about your future?

What have you believed about yourself that isn't

true?

What have you believed about yourself that isn't true?

1.

2.

3.

4.

5.

What have you believed about yourself that isn't

true?

What have you believed about yourself that isn't true?

What are 3-5 things you do to improve your mood?

What are 3-5 things you do to improve your mood?

1.

2.

3.

4.

5.

What are 3-5 things you do to improve your mood?

What are 3-5 things you do to improve your mood?

What do you do to nourish your mind?

What do you do to nourish your mind?

1.

2.

3.

4.

5.

What do you do to nourish your mind?

What do you do to nourish your mind?

What are 3-5 negative thoughts about yourself that
you need to release?

What are 3-5 negative thoughts about yourself that you need to release?

1.

2.

3.

4.

5.

What are 3-5 negative thoughts about yourself that
you need to release?

What are 3-5 thoughts about yourself that you need to release?

What are the lies that your inner critic tells you?

What are the lies that your inner critic tells you?

1.

2.

3.

4.

5.

What are the lies that your inner critic tells you?

What are the lies that your inner critic tells you?

What is stopping you from being disciplined?

What is stopping you from being disciplined?

1.

2.

3.

4.

5.

What is stopping you from being disciplined?

What is stopping you from being disciplined?

What do you do when you need to apologize to yourself?

What do you do when you need to apologize to yourself?

1.

2.

3.

4.

5.

What do you do when you need to apologize to yourself?

What do you do when you need to apologize to yourself?

What habits do I need to start and commit to?

What habits do I need to start and commit to?

1.

2.

3.

4.

5.

What habits do I need to start and commit to?

What habits do I need to start and commit to?

What are you most proud of?

What are you most proud of?

1.

2.

3.

4.

5.

What are you most proud of?

What are you most proud of?

What do you do to make a difference in the lives of others?

What do you do to make a difference in the lives of others?

1.

2.

3.

4.

5.

What do you do to make a difference in the lives of others?

What do you do to make a difference in the lives of others?

When did you start to forget about yourself?

When did you start to forget about yourself?

1.

2.

3.

4.

5.

When did you start to forget about yourself?

When did you start to forget about yourself?

When did you find your personal freedom?

When did you find your personal freedom?

1.

2.

3.

4.

5.

When did you find your personal freedom?

When did you find your personal freedom?

When was the last time you said something kind to yourself?

When was the last time you said something kind to yourself?

1.

2.

3.

4.

5.

When was the last time you said something kind to

yourself?

When was the last time you said something kind to yourself?

When was the last time you did something nice for
yourself?

When was the last time you did something nice for yourself?

1.

2.

3.

4.

5.

When was the last time you did something nice for yourself?

When was the last time you did something nice for
yourself?

Where does your true happiness come from?

Where does your true happiness come from?

1.

2.

3.

4.

5.

Where does your true happiness come from?

Where does your true happiness come from?

Who makes you anxious?

Who makes you anxious?

1.

2.

3.

4.

5.

Who makes you anxious?

Who makes you anxious?

Who do you need to forgive?

Who do you need to forgive?

1.

2.

3.

4.

5.

Who do you need to forgive?

Who do you need to forgive?

Body

WRITING PROMPTS FOR THE BODY

I love my body because__.

I love my body because__.

1.

2.

3.

4.

5.

I love my body because___.

I love my body because__.

How do you feel about your body right now?

How do you feel about your body right now?

1.

2.

3.

4.

5.

How do you feel about your body right now?

How do you feel about your body right now?

Do you connect your self-worth with how you feel about your body?

Do you connect your self-worth with how you feel about your body?

1.

2.

3.

4.

5.

Do you connect your self-worth with how you feel about your body?

Do you connect your self-worth with how you feel about your body?

Have a conversation with your body, what did you
say?

Have a conversation with your body, what did you say?

1.

2.

3.

4.

5.

Have a conversation with your body, what did you say?

Have a conversation with your body, what did you say?

What are three to five ways you can nourish your body?

What are three to five ways you can nourish your body?

1.

2.

3.

4.

5.

What are three to five ways you can nourish your body?

What are three to five ways you can nourish your body?

How does your body respond to consistent movement?

How does your body respond to consistent movement?

1.

2.

3.

4.

5.

How does your body respond to consistent

movement?

How does your body respond to consistent movement?

At this moment my body needs __.

At this moment my body needs __.

1.

2.

3.

4.

5.

At this moment my body needs __.

At this moment my body needs __.

I feel ___ when I exercise.

I feel ___ when I exercise.

1.

2.

3.

4.

5.

I feel ___ when I exercise.

I feel ___ when I exercise.

When I think of exercise I__.

When I think of exercise I__.

1.

2.

3.

4.

5.

When I think of exercise I__.

When I think of exercise I__.

When you think of your body what is the first
thing that comes to mind?

When you think of your body what is the first thing that comes to mind?

1.

2.

3.

4.

5.

When you think of your body what is the first
thing that comes to mind?

When you think of your body what is the first
thing that comes to mind?

What are some ways you can treat your body better?

What are some ways you can treat your body better?

1.

2.

3.

4.

5.

What are some ways you can treat your body better?

What are some ways you can treat your body better?

Your stomach wants to tell you something what is it?

Your stomach wants to tell you something what is it?

1.

2.

3.

4.

5.

Your stomach wants to tell you something what is
it?

Your stomach wants to tell you something what is
it?

The last time you listened to your gut, what happened?

The last time you listened to your gut, what happened?

1.

2.

3.

4.

5.

The last time you listened to your gut, what happened?

The last time you listened to your gut, what happened?

What makes you feel beautiful?

What makes you feel beautiful?

1.

2.

3.

4.

5.

What makes you feel beautiful?

What makes you feel beautiful?

What is your favorite comfort food?

What is your favorite comfort food?

1.

2.

3.

4.

5.

What is your favorite comfort food?

What is your favorite comfort food?

How do you pamper yourself?

How do you pamper yourself?

1.

2.

3.

4.

5.

How do you pamper yourself?

How do you pamper yourself?

Your body is holding a story that needs to be
released, what is it?

Your body is holding a story that needs to be released, what is it?

1.

2.

3.

4.

5.

Your body is holding a story that needs to be
released, what is it?

Your body is holding a story that needs to be released, what is it?

Your feet are planted in the place of your dreams,

where are you?

Your feet are planted in the place of your dreams, where are you?

1.

2.

3.

4.

5.

Your feet are planted in the place of your dreams, where are you?

Your feet are planted in the place of your dreams, where are you?

When I take a deep breath, my body whispers__.

When I take a deep breath, my body whispers___.

1.

2.

3.

4.

5.

When I take a deep breath, my body whispers___.

When I take a deep breath, my body whispers___.

My spirit is telling me a vision that is nothing close to my present reality. What is it?

My spirit is telling me a vision that is nothing close
to my present reality. What is it?

1.

2.

3.

4.

5.

My spirit is telling me a vision that is nothing close
to my present reality. What is it?

My spirit is telling me a vision that is nothing close to my present reality. What is it?

I love _____ (body part) because__.

I love _____ (body part) because__.

1.

2.

3.

4.

5.

I love _____ (body part) because___.

I love _____ (body part) because__.

I appreciate my body because_____.

I appreciate my body because_____.

1.

2.

3.

4.

5.

I appreciate my body because_____.

I appreciate my body because_____.

Your body shows up for you daily. How do you show it gratitude and appreciation?

Your body shows up for you daily. How do you show it gratitude and appreciation?

1.

2.

3.

4.

5.

Your body shows up for you daily. How do you
show it gratitude and appreciation?

Your body shows up for you daily. How do you show it gratitude and appreciation?

What are three to five things you love about your

body?

What are three to five things you love about your body?

1.

2.

3.

4.

5.

What are three to five things you love about your body?

What are three to five things you love about your body?

How does stress feel in your body?

How does stress feel in your body?

1.

2.

3.

4.

5.

How does stress feel in your body?

How does stress feel in your body?

How does happiness feel in your body?

How does happiness feel in your body?

1.

2.

3.

4.

5.

How does happiness feel in your body?

How does happiness feel in your body?

When I overeat, I am feeding____.

When I overeat, I am feeding___.

1.

2.

3.

4.

5.

When I overeat, I am feeding___.

When I overeat, I am feeding____.

What are some ways you can treat your body better?

What are some ways you can treat your body better?

1.

2.

3.

4.

5.

What are some ways you can treat your body better?

What are some ways you can treat your body better?

I will do less of_____ to keep my body healthy.

I will do less of_____ to keep my body healthy.

1.

2.

3.

4.

5.

I will do less of_____ to keep my body healthy.

I will do less of_____ to keep my body healthy.

I feel most energized when I__.

I feel most energized when I__.

1.

2.

3.

4.

5.

I feel most energized when I___.

I feel most energized when I__.

Soul

WRITING PROMPTS FOR THE SOUL

Your heart has a message, what is it?

Your heart has a message, what is it?

1.

2.

3.

4.

5.

Your heart has a message, what is it?

Your heart has a message, what is it?

Tears that will not come to surface have to do with_.

Tears that will not come to surface have to do with_.

1.

2.

3.

4.

5.

Tears that will not come to surface have to do with_.

Tears that will not come to surface have to do with_.

In what ways are you disrespecting yourself?

In what ways are you disrespecting yourself?

1.

2.

3.

4.

5.

In what ways are you disrespecting yourself?

In what ways are you disrespecting yourself?

I owe my younger self an apology, what is it?

I owe my younger self an apology, what is it?

1.

2.

3.

4.

5.

I owe my younger self an apology, what is it?

I owe my younger self an apology, what is it?

The self-sabotaging behavior I need to stop is____.

The self-sabotaging behavior I need to stop is____.

1.

2.

3.

4.

5.

The self-sabotaging behavior I need to stop is___.

The self-sabotaging behavior I need to stop is____.

I lost myself when I said yes to__.

I lost myself when I said yes to__.

1.

2.

3.

4.

5.

I lost myself when I said yes to___.

I lost myself when I said yes to__.

The unhealthy habit I use to comfort myself is___.

The unhealthy habit I use to comfort myself is___.

1.

2.

3.

4.

5.

The unhealthy habit I use to comfort myself is___.

The unhealthy habit I use to comfort myself is__.

What can you do today that will bring you closer to

your dream?

What can you do today that will bring you closer to your dream?

1.

2.

3.

4.

5.

What can you do today that will bring you closer

to your dream?

What can you do today that will bring you closer to
your dream?

I am grateful for_.

I am grateful for_.

1.

2.

3.

4.

5.

I am grateful for_.

I am grateful for_.

Do you feel supported?

Do you feel supported?

1.

2.

3.

4.

5.

Do you feel supported?

Do you feel supported?

How can you communicate your needs more effectively?

How can you communicate your needs more effectively?

1.

2.

3.

4.

5.

How can you communicate your needs more
effectively?

How can you communicate your needs more
effectively?

How do you show yourself respect?

How do you show yourself respect?

1.

2.

3.

4.

5.

How do you show yourself respect?

How do you show yourself respect?

What do you do to comfort your soul when it is tired?

What do you do to comfort your soul when it is tired?

1.

2.

3.

4.

5.

What do you do to comfort your soul when it is tired?

What do you do to comfort your soul when it is tired?

If you loved yourself unconditionally, what would
your life look like?

If you loved yourself unconditionally, what would your life look like?

1.

2.

3.

4.

5.

If you loved yourself unconditionally, what would your life look like?

If you loved yourself unconditionally, what would your life look like?

I would like to say "no" to these things, but I don't.
What are they?

I would like to say "no" to these things, but I don't.
What are they?

1.

2.

3.

4.

5.

I would like to say "no" to these things, but I don't. What are they?

I would like to say "no" to these things, but I don't.
What are they?

What is a compliment that you are given often, but
don't believe?

What is a compliment that you are given often, but don't believe?

1.

2.

3.

4.

5.

What is a compliment that you are given often, but
don't believe?

What is a compliment that you are given often, but don't believe?

What is a childhood memory that needs healing?

What is a childhood memory that needs healing?

1.

2.

3.

4.

5.

What is a childhood memory that needs healing?

What is a childhood memory that needs healing?

What was your favorite song in high school?

What was your favorite song in high school?

1.

2.

3.

4.

5.

What was your favorite song in high school?

What was your favorite song in high school?

What do others see in you that you don't see in
yourself?

What do others see in you that you don't see in yourself?

1.

2.

3.

4.

5.

What do others see in you that you don't see in yourself?

What do others see in you that you don't see in yourself?

What do you need to do to for yourself to feel supported?

What do you need to do to for yourself to feel supported?

1.

2.

3.

4.

5.

What do you need to do to for yourself to feel supported?

What do you need to do to for yourself to feel supported?

What do you need from others to feel supported?

What do you need from others to feel supported?

1.

2.

3.

4.

5.

What do you need from others to feel supported?

What do you need from others to feel supported?

What truth do you need to tell yourself?

What truth do you need to tell yourself?

1.

2.

3.

4.

5.

What truth do you need to tell yourself?

What truth do you need to tell yourself?

You are responsible for your peace and happiness,
how are you taking personal responsibility?

You are responsible for your peace and happiness, how are you taking personal responsibility?

1.

2.

3.

4.

5.

You are responsible for your peace and happiness,
how are you taking personal responsibility?

You are responsible for your peace and happiness, how are you taking personal responsibility?

How do you set personal boundaries?

How do you set personal boundaries?

1.

2.

3.

4.

5.

How do you set personal boundaries?

How do you set personal boundaries?

I have a hard time saying no to this person

because___.

I have a hard time saying no to this person because____.

1.

2.

3.

4.

5.

I have a hard time saying no to this person
because___.

I have a hard time saying no to this person because____.

What brings tears to your eyes?

What brings tears to your eyes?

1.

2.

3.

4.

5.

What brings tears to your eyes?

What brings tears to your eyes?

Do you know your purpose?

Do you know your purpose?

1.

2.

3.

4.

5.

Do you know your purpose?

Do you know your purpose?

What external thing do you attach your self-worth
to?

What external thing do you attach your self-worth to?

1.

2.

3.

4.

5.

What external thing do you attach your self-worth to?

What external thing do you attach your self-worth to?

Do you feel like you are not enough? If so, who made you feel that way? What would make you feel like you are more than enough?

Do you feel like you are not enough? If so, who made you feel that way? What would make you feel like you are more than enough?

1.

2.

3.

4.

5.

Do you feel like you are not enough? If so, who made you feel that way? What would make you feel like you are more than enough?

Do you feel like you are not enough? If so, who made you feel that way? What would make you feel like you are more than enough?

Who is the person inside of you that you want the world to see?

Who is the person inside of you that you want the world to see?

1.

2.

3.

4.

5.

Who is the person inside of you that you want the world to see?

Who is the person inside of you that you want the world to see?

Do you show love to others more than you do to yourself?

Do you show love to others more than you do to yourself?

1.

2.

3.

4.

5.

Do you show love to others more than you do to yourself?

Do you show love to others more than you do to yourself?

What do you value outside of yourself that makes

you feel complete?

What do you value outside of yourself that makes you feel complete?

1.

2.

3.

4.

5.

What do you value outside of yourself that makes you feel complete?

What do you value outside of yourself that makes you feel complete?

How are you showing up for yourself daily to live
your best life?

How are you showing up for yourself daily to live your best life?

1.

2.

3.

4.

5.

How are you showing up for yourself daily to live your best life?

How are you showing up for yourself daily to live your best life?

About the Author

Yvelette Stines is a writer and educator. Her work has been published in Essence, Black Enterprise, Heart and Soul, The Root, The Source, Mind Body + Green, Purely Delicious Raw, Green Build + Design and more. She coaches and teaches workshops to both children and adults on writing and wellness. Stines has a B.A. in Communication Studies, an M.Ed in Education, and M.S. Holistic Nutrition.

To learn more visit www.yvelettestines.com.

Other Titles

Written by Yvelette Stines

Vernon the Vegetable Man

Be Calm: 31 Mindful Affirmations and Reflections for Living a Peaceful Life

Available on www.yvelettestines.com.

www.ingramcontent.com/pod-product-compliance
Lightning Source LLC
Chambersburg PA
CBHW050612300426

44112CB00012B/1465